ACKNOWLEDGEMENT

We acknowledge the many health professionals involved with the American Association for Health Education, the Society for Public Health Education and the National Commission for Health Education Credentialing, Inc., dedicated to the pursuit of excellence in health education professional preparation at the undergraduate and graduate levels.

ISBN #: 0-9652570-2-9

TABLE OF CONTENTS

Appendices

INTRODUCTION AND THE RATIONALE FOR A TRANSITIONAL DOCUMENT

This document builds on "Standards for the Preparation of Graduate-Level Health Educators" published in 1997, by including expanded content descriptions and objectives for the graduate level competencies. This specificity is intended to assist professional preparation programs in adapting their curricula and practitioners in identifying their continuing education needs. The competencies were developed by the profession for the profession and have been embraced by the National Commission for Health Education Credentialing, Inc., (NCHEC), the Council on Education for Public Health and other groups.

Although identification and publication of the graduate level competencies helps advance the profession, it is also acknowledged that such competencies may need to be updated over time to keep pace with changes and developments in the field. One such development is NCHEC's re-verification of the entry-level competencies and sub-competencies, which will take place in 1999 and 2000. It is possible that the competency update project will identify changes to be made to the entry-level competencies, and hence trigger modifications to the graduate level competencies. In the meantime, it is important to disseminate the advanced-level competencies so that the health education profession can begin to use them. This 1999 document will serve to bridge the transition period until the role re-verification study and validation of the new graduate competencies is complete, at which time new documents will be considered for publication.

EVOLUTION OF HEALTH EDUCATION COMPETENCIES

Health education, a profession of practitioners, academicians, and researchers dedicated to defining and developing a field of practice in service to society, has been evolving for three-quarters of a century. As a part of this evolution, the profession of health education has a long history of graduate professional preparation. For example, at a 1950 conference sponsored by the American Association for Health, Physical Education, and Recreation (AAHPER), graduate standards for health education teachers were among the recommendations (Athletic Institute, 1950). Criteria and guidelines for accrediting graduate programs in community health education were published in the March 1969 edition of the *American Journal of Public Health* (APHA, 1969). An example of the extensive involvement of the profession at the graduate level was the requirement of a Master of Public Health degree for membership in the Society for Public Health Education (SOPHE). Building on these foundations of tradition, introspection, and vision, concerned professionals during the late 1970s and 1980s delineated and validated the roles and responsibilities of health educators to improve professional preparation and practice at the entry-level.

Entry-level competencies provide a foundation for professional preparation, which may be acquired as early as the undergraduate level. As the entry-level competencies were implemented in professional preparation, certification, and accreditation, the need for a profession-wide set of graduate-level standards was recognized. Bensley & Pope (1992) discussed inconsistencies in graduate-level health education preparation. For example, they found that a research methods course was required in less than 60 percent of all schools preparing graduate health educators.

This narrative reviews the history of the development of graduate-level responsibilities and competencies for the health education profession. Underlying assumptions are presented, as well as the chronology of the graduate competency development process.

Maintaining and assuring quality professional preparation and practice in health education has been an increasing concern to the profession. A brief review of history helps put into perspective the events that have brought the profession to focus on the need to define competencies for graduate preparation that can be applied across all settings.

Some of the early guidelines for health educators were developed by the professional associations, including the American Association for Health Education (AAHE); the Society for Public Health Education (SOPHE); and the American Public Health Association's (APHA's) Public Health Education and Health Promotion, and School Health Education & Services sections. Professional education of health educators was promoted as early as 1943 (Creswell, 1981). The AAHPER developed guidelines for teacher education (1969), and safety and school health education (1974). Other professional health education organizations, including the American School Health Association (ASHA, 1976) and SOPHE (Creswell, 1981; SOPHE, 1977), promulgated guidelines and recommendations throughout the 1970s.

In February 1978, the First Bethesda Conference brought together health educators from all practice settings to begin the process of defining and verifying the role of the health educator in all health education practice settings. Their recommendation that a national task force be established for the preparation and practice of health educators was realized in March 1978, when the National Center for Health Education undertook the initial Role Delineation Project (Department of Health, Education & Welfare, 1978).

In January 1980 the final draft of the initial role delineation report was completed (USDHHS, 1980). Phase II of the project involved the role verification and refinement process (Henderson & McIntosh, 1981). Surveys of practitioners, interview data and regional discussion groups were used to determine the relationship of the proposed competencies to actual practice. Respondents in the field verified that a generic role was common and appropriate for health educators in all five settings, whether school, university, community, medical care or workplace. At approximately the same time, colleges and universities offering degrees in health education were surveyed about their curricula. Results verified a lack of consistency throughout professional preparation programs.

It became increasingly evident that a common framework was essential for the academic preparation of health educators. With this thought in mind, the National Conference for Institutions Preparing Health Educators was convened in Birmingham, Alabama, in February 1981 (USDHHS, 1981). It became clear that the profession needed competency-based curricula consistent with the delineated and verified generic roles and responsibilities. Input from the academic program representatives at Birmingham was used to refine the roles and responsibilities. In 1983, a draft framework was developed that included seven areas of responsibility and their competencies and sub-competencies (Mathews, 1983). A revision of this document, called "A Framework for the Development of Competency-Based Curricula for Entry-Level Health Educators," was released in 1985 by the National Task Force, but later came to be known simply as the "Framework."

In 1986, a second Bethesda conference provided consensus that a "certification process" was appropriate to ensure that those individuals delivering health education services had obtained the minimal level of competency. In June 1988, the National Task Force on the Preparation and Practice of Health Educators, Inc., became the National Commission for Health Education Credentialing (NCHEC). Members of the National Task Force became an Interim Board of Commissioners initially charged to define the credentialing mission for NCHEC. This marked the beginning of a new era addressing the credentialing process in health education. The professional literature reflects the extended debates over the definition of entry-level, the applicability of competencies to all practice settings and the inclusion or absence of specific topical health-related content within the competencies (see references for suggested readings).

Before a credentialing process could be established, agreement was necessary on a common body of knowledge, skills and competencics, which must then be validated. Using the seven areas of responsibility for entry-level health educators developed by the National Task Force on the Preparation and Practice of Health Education, the NCHEC began granting the Certified Health Education Specialist (CHES) credential in 1989. In 1990 the first group of individuals received the CHES credential through successful completion of a criterion-referenced examination, based on the Framework. This nationwide testing program was a landmark event in the profession. As of October 1998, over 5000 individuals are active CHES, the CHES examination is given twice a year and some employers are requiring/preferring the CHES credential in job announcements.

Well before NCHEC formally initiated its role in the credentialing of individual entry-level health educators, professional associations had established processes to accredit or approve professional preparation programs. The APHA, responsible for accrediting schools of public health since the mid-1940s, implemented a formal accreditation process for graduate community health education programs, and in 1969 APHA accredited the first such program outside a school of public health. Today, accreditation or approval processes are carried out in several venues. Beginning in 1988, the AAHE served as the learned society for health education, providing recommendations on compliance with guidelines for school health education professional preparation programs through the accreditation process of the National Council for Accreditation of Teacher Education (NCATE). In 1980 the SOPHE initiated a review procedure for baccalaureate programs in community health education, but in 1984 SOPHE joined with AAHE to sponsor a single review process, now implemented through the SOPHE/AAHE Baccalaureate Program Approval Committee (SABPAC). Both AAHE/NCATE and SABPAC processes currently rely on the entry-level competencies as part of the criteria for program review. The Council on Education for Public Health (CEPH) assumed the accreditation responsibilities from APHA in 1974. CEPH accredits graduate community health education programs which offer the MPH or other public health degrees, although the vast majority of non-MPH programs in health education are not accredited. The CEPH graduate-level criteria rely on early work of APHA, but also on the work of SOPHE, which in 1967 adopted a statement on the functions of community health educators at both the bachelors and masters levels.

The efforts of many individuals and professional organizations have helped to refine and clarify what is expected from professionally prepared entry-level health educators. There now exists a set of clearly defined responsibilities and competencies that guide academic curricula, form the basis of program approval processes, and provide the core criteria for the health education specialist examination.

Although a credentialing process exists for entry-level health educators and approval processes are in place for entry-level preparation programs, more limited attention has been directed at the advanced level of health education practice. In 1967, SOPHE published a "Statement of Functions of Community Health Educators and Minimum Requirements for their Professional Preparation, with Recommendations for Implementation." This document provided guidelines to universities and community employers on the role of community health educators at the baccalaureate level, functioning under the direction of a master's level professional health educator (SOPHE, 1967). Subsequently, in 1975, SOPHE published "Guidelines for the Preparation and Practice of Professional Health Educators" to provide direction for the master's level health education specialist and to serve as a partial basis for the accreditation of health education teaching programs and/or national certification (SOPHE, 1977). The profession's early efforts to define the knowledge base and identify the competencies needed to perform at the advanced practitioner level had not been subjected to the same level of analysis and validation as had the entry-level competencies. It was several decades later, in 1992, that SOPHE and AAHE, at the request of NCATE and other groups, organized a joint committee to address defining graduate-level competencies for professional practice, which could impact professional preparation programs as well as further credentialing efforts. Many health educators recognized that a framework for the advanced practitioner also would provide knowledge and an organized set of skills for developing continuing education and training programs for health educators.

CHRONOLOGY OF THE GRADUATE COMPETENCY DEVELOPMENT PROCESS

The Joint Committee for Graduate Standards was established by AAHE and SOPHE in 1992. The original committee membership was drawn from members of the AAHE/NCATE and SABPAC Review Committees. Letters were sent to all health education professional organizations belonging to the Coalition of National Health Education Organizations, inviting their participation in the process. Because AAHE and SOPHE already had representatives on the Committee, they were considered founding members of this new undertaking, and therefore committed financial support to the project.

The Joint Committee's daunting challenge was to build upon the entry-level competencies by answering the question, "If the practitioner already has health education training and is extending that education with advanced training, what MORE do they need in the way of advanced competencies?" (Mail, 1996). Further, the Joint Committee was working with a copyrighted document and was therefore unable to make any revisions in the entry-level competencies.

In October 1992, the Joint Committee met in a two-day retreat to determine how best to proceed. The development of these competencies was guided by a number of assumptions generated by the Joint Committee, including the following:

- The entry-level roles, responsibilities and competencies reflect undergraduate preparation. At completion of a graduate-level program, a student should possess those entry-level competencies in addition to the graduate-level competencies.

- The newly developed responsibilities and competencies are for graduate-level preparation. Inherent in advanced preparation competencies are higher cognitive processes such as analysis, synthesis, and evaluation. Consequently, more abstract terms such as "appropriate" and "effective" are used rather than the term describing more concrete, defined benchmarks of competency.

The Joint Committee recognized that the development and refinement of roles and competencies is an ongoing process involving many segments of the health education profession.

During discussions on this process, three outcomes were identified:

1. Graduate competencies would be developed that build on the competencies and sub-competencies for entry-level preparation.

2. Additional responsibilities and competencies would be identified that reflected preparation at the advanced level of education.

3. Where appropriate, new sub-competencies would be added to the existing and newly developed responsibilities and competencies.

The Committee first proposed new graduate level responsibilities, competencies and sub-competencies. During the remainder of 1992 and the beginning of 1993, a survey instrument was developed to invite input and elicit feedback from practitioners. By October 1993, using the lists of names provided by universities, the Committee sent the instrument to 418 practitioners drawn from higher education, health departments, work sites, and school health departments. The Committee compiled and reviewed the responses in April 1994. Comments from this first survey were used to further modify the instrument.

From the beginning of the process, the widest inclusion of professional representation was necessary. This became even more apparent as time passed, so the committee asked for and received representation from the CEPH and the NCHEC. With the added input and perspective of these new members (see Appendix B), the draft was further refined in late 1994 and early 1995. A second draft was prepared and mailed to institutions with graduate-level professional preparation in health education for their input and reactions. Results of this survey were reported at the annual AAHE meeting in March 1995, and the response to this report from professionals attending the meeting was predominately positive.

The Committee met in July 1995 to consider final revisions of the recommended changes and new responsibilities and competencies. A National Congress for Institutions Preparing Graduate Health Educators was convened in Dallas, Texas, in February 1996. The purpose of this Congress, comprising 138 representatives and 81 institutions, was to obtain direct input from all institutions preparing masters and doctoral level health educators.

The charge to the conferees was to: (1) review the proposed graduate additions to the curriculum framework; (2) make recommendations for the implementation and adoption of competencies; (3) develop recommendations for application of these graduate competencies; and (4) increase professional solidarity for the preparation of practitioners. The response from participants was overwhelmingly positive about both the meeting and the general concept.

At the 1996 AAHE annual meeting, the Committee met to incorporate feedback from the National Congress. The refined document then was distributed to all participants attending the National Congress, as well as to those program administrators not represented in Dallas. This second round of feedback conveyed broad acceptance of the concept and substance of the proposed graduate competencies. The final meeting of the Committee, in July 1996, resulted in completion of the initial report to AAHE and SOPHE. This report included the National Congress Proceedings; the Refined Graduate Responsibilities, Competencies and Sub-competencies; a glossary and recommendations to the profession. In addition, the Committee facilitated presentations and dialogue on the proposed responsibilities and competencies at both the 1996 AAHE annual meeting and the 1996 SOPHE midyear and annual meetings. The presentations included discussions concerning implications for professional preparation and practice.

The Joint Committee submitted its final report to the Boards of AAHE and SOPHE in July 1996. The AAHE Board of Directors accepted this report and graduate competencies recommendations in October 1996 and the SOPHE Board of Trustees approved the graduate competencies in November 1996. Additionally, the NCHEC's Board of Commissioners endorsed the competencies in July 1997. Information about the competencies was disseminated widely to all the professional organizations, as well as to various governmental agencies. SOPHE and AAHE formed the Graduate Standards Implementation Committee in July 1997 with representatives from NCHEC, SABPAC, NCATE, CEPH and the Association of Schools of Public Health (ASPH) (see Appendix C).

As a first step in implementation of the graduate competencies standards, a representative group of individuals formed the Graduate Standards Ad-Hoc Writing Committee (see Appendix D) and was charged with clarifying the language and formatting the graduate competencies in a manner similar to the entry-level competencies. As a means of clarification and a mechanism for illustrating the generic applicability of these new competencies and sub-competencies, expanded content descriptions and objectives were developed. The Ad-Hoc Writing Committee completed its task in October 1997.

The Writing Committee asked the Implementation Committee to address the following issues: using the term "competencies" rather than "standards" in all future documents, resolving copyright issues, determining the appropriate format to integrate the new competencies within the existing competencies and deciding whether "advanced practitioner" was meant to include masters and doctoral levels of preparation.

The Graduate Competencies Implementation Committee met in November 1997 and agreed upon the following items:

- The word "standards" was to be removed from any language used to describe the new graduate level responsibilities, competencies and sub-competencies. "Standards" implies program criteria; the Implementation Committee acknowledged that program criteria could incorporate these new competencies. However, these competencies are guidelines for advanced level practitioners.

- The Writing Committee had recommended identifying the Graduate Responsibilities, Competencies and Sub-competencies as masters level, but the Implementation Committee differed in its opinion. Members came to a consensus to keep the graduate competencies generic and applicable to anyone pursuing an advanced degree in health education. Members further acknowledged that this issue may need to be revisited.

Since the new competencies and sub-competencies were added to the existing area of responsibilities, these competencies may not align well in a hierarchical order originally conceptualized for the framework. Members agreed this task would be considered at a later date.

BENEFITS OF GRADUATE LEVEL RESPONSIBILITIES AND COMPETENCIES

There are many benefits of articulating graduate responsibilities, competencies, and sub-competencies.

Foremost is the identification of a common core knowledge and skills base that define health educators as an occupation and lend recognition to health education as a distinct profession. The graduate competencies for health educators reflect a higher level of professional functioning, as evidenced in the three added responsibilities of research, administration and the advancement of the profession, along with additional and expanded competencies and sub-competencies for the seven entry-level responsibilities. Since the development of skills in these areas of responsibility should be addressed in graduate-level academic programs, the graduate competencies can guide curricular design and program revisions. For example, the graduate competencies can form the core of a graduate program in health education, around which appropriate courses and other learning experiences can be designed. Overall, the graduate competencies can help guide accreditation, training and certification.

Individuals who pursue graduate education that is focused on the graduate competencies will benefit from a framework in which employment and continuing education opportunities are defined. Continuing education experiences can focus on specific responsibilities and related competencies and sub-competencies for professional enhancement. These ongoing skill-development opportunities can be of eventual benefit to the various groups served by the health educator.

Importantly, in 1998 the U.S. Departments of Commerce and Labor formally acknowledged "health educator" as a distinct occupation. Such recognition was justified, based to a large extent, on the ability of the profession to specify its unique skills. In 1997, Arkansas established a Board of Health Education for the regulation of the practice of health educators in the State. The law requires most health educators in Arkansas to be CHES, resulting in a registry of CHES professionals. Job announcements for health educators offered by the State of California, as well as by private employers, increasingly indicate a preference for individuals with a CHES credential. This type of external recognition is largely based upon the profession's ability to clarify its distinctive roles and responsibilities. With continuity, promotion and education, it can be assumed that such recognition will only expand in the future.

IMPLICATIONS OF THE GRADUATE RESPONSIBILITIES AND COMPETENCIES

The driving force for developing the responsibilities and competencies was the need for standards to guide professional preparation programs. However, the responsibilities and competencies can serve as a foundation for other forms of credentialing. Health education credentialing includes the certification of individuals and the accreditation of professional preparation programs. A component of the credentialing system is the requirement of continuing education for certified individuals and those interested in improving their professional practice. As Helen Cleary (1995) notes, "...a credentialing process is not the total answer to anyone's problems, but it can improve the quality of professional preparation and of professional practice. It can also help a profession organize itself. But none of this is possible unless the profession is willing to work to make it happen" (Cleary, p. vii).

There are two obvious implications for the adoption of graduate professional preparation competencies. The first is to assure that, regardless of the university or college from which an individual graduates, there is a common core of preparation for practice upon which employers can rely. The more that professional preparation is recognized as adhering to nationally acknowledged competencies, the more health education will be recognized as a profession, and the more marketable will be every program's graduates. A secondary implication is that the faculty in professional preparation programs will exhibit the broad range of experience and training that contributes to the competencies. As competencies are adopted, they will be integrated into accreditation standards or program approval review procedures and individual certification programs.

The profession of health education is at a juncture of unprecedented opportunity, in part defined by its own efforts to enhance the skills and abilities of the health education practitioner, but also by the dramatic changes occurring nationwide that are related to the organization, delivery and payment of health services. These changes are driven by a variety of considerations, but all embrace the concept that education and behavior change are critical to our nation's ability to achieve an optimal level of health. This recognition results in a myriad of opportunities for health educators, some in very traditional roles, some in new roles and some in roles that are only now emerging. Although professional career options for health education employment are quite varied, they share a common base of knowledge related to how people learn and make decisions about health. In addition they all utilize basic educational theories and principles, behavioral science concepts, and knowledge about the biological basis of disease and health. The health educator of the future will draw on a broad array of effective teaching methods and techniques.

There are many other potential uses for these graduate competencies, such as developing a certification exam at the advanced level of practice. Practitioners could find the competencies useful in assessing their needs for continuing education. Finally, the profession could employ the graduate competencies as a component of graduate standards to accredit or approve graduate programs. Academic institutions, professional organizations, and accreditation agencies can adopt the competencies and strengthen professional preparation programs. Employers and legislators can use the graduate competencies to establish criteria for jobs in health education.

NEXT STEPS FOR THE PROFESSION

Nationwide distribution of this document will provide an opportunity for graduate programs and health education professionals to begin to use the responsibilities, competencies and sub-competencies as guidelines for accreditation, training and certification. Of note, as the implementation process for the graduate competencies takes place, NCHEC is preparing to re-verify the current entry-level responsibilities and competencies. This process, facilitated by the Competency Update Project committee, also will include validation of the graduate level responsibilities and competencies during 1999 and 2000. Still many issues will need to be resolved by the field. For example, should a certification process be developed at the graduate level; if so, how would this process differ for those already certified at the entry-level in contrast to those who are not yet certified?

THREE NEW AREAS OF GRADUATE RESPONSIBILITY

Three new Areas of Responsibility were proposed by the Joint Committee. In addition, advanced competencies and sub-competencies were added, where appropriate, to the original seven Areas of Responsibility.

1. Applying Appropriate Research Principles and Techniques in Health Education

Generally at the graduate level, students master the skills of data collection and analysis, as well as a greater understanding of formulating recommendations for program development, revision, and/or maintenance based upon their research findings. The Joint Committee developed this eighth Area of Responsibility, (containing 3 specific competencies and 14 sub-competencies) to assure that graduate level curricula for health educators reflect the appropriate quality of research principles, including competency in applying quantitative and qualitative data.

2. Administering Health Education Programs

In some practice areas, graduate-level health educators assume significant management responsibilities. In other practice areas, supervision of staff comes with increased experience and responsibility. The Joint Committee framed this ninth Area of Responsibility to reflect the need for management and supervisory skills required for future employment and career advancement. This area of responsibility is delineated by 4 competencies and 16 sub-competencies.

3. Advancing the Profession of Health Education

A major responsibility of a graduate-prepared health education professional is to provide leadership services to individuals and organizations in an ethical manner (SOPHE and AAHE Codes of Ethics) (AAHE, 1994; SOPHE, 1983). Graduate preparation programs commonly imbue students with increased competency in leadership skills, as well as professional socialization. The Joint Committee created this tenth Area of Responsibility with 3 competencies and 8 sub-competencies reflecting quality in leadership knowledge and skills, advocacy and cognition of ethical principles to guide the practice of health education.

New competencies and sub-competencies added to the existing seven areas of responsibility are listed on the following page.

Competencies and Sub-Competencies
Additions to Existing Framework

In addition to the new areas of responsibility, new competencies and sub-competencies reflecting advanced practitioner skills were incorporated into the existing entry-level framework by these revisions:

Area of Responsibility I: Assessing Individual and Community Needs for Health Education

Added: 1 new competency and 5 new sub-competencies

Area of Responsibility II: Planning Effective Health Education Programs

Added: 1 new competency and 8 new sub-competencies

Area of Responsibility III: Implementing Health Education Programs

Added: 6 new sub-competencies

Area of Responsibility IV: Evaluating Effectiveness of Health Education Programs

Added: 11 new sub-competencies

Area of Responsibility V: Coordinating Provision of Health Education Services

Added: 2 new sub-competencies

Area of Responsibility VI: Acting as a Resource Person in Health Education

Added: 5 new sub-competencies

Area of Responsibility VII: Communicating Health and Health Education Needs, Concerns and Resources

Added: 6 new sub-competencies

DESCRIPTORS OF ROLES

AREA OF RESPONSIBILITY VIII
Applying Appropriate Research Principles and Techniques in Health Education

The Role

Health educators at the advanced level are expected to be able to conduct a thorough review of the literature and to apply research findings to advance the profession. The advanced competencies include the ability to select appropriate qualitative and quantitative methodologies, to interpret results, and to apply findings to health education practice.

Health educators may be expected to write applications for funding, including research proposals. The ability to apply research design to new and developing programs in order to assess effectiveness is important in justifying program continuance and to maintain funding in an increasingly competitive work environment. In addition, the aggregation of data from one or multiple programs for the purpose of establishing baselines and making comparisons is important. Drawing widely from various measures to establish the economic contributions or impacts of health education and health promotion programs, advanced level health educators help identify other professionals needed for collaborative approaches as well as provide information to governments, employers, and program funding sources. In addition, translation of research findings into lay language helps make health communications more credible.

Community Setting - The health educator may use epidemiological principles to explain disease outbreaks or define high-risk neighborhoods within communities that require special program emphasis. Outcome data may provide necessary information to support programs when reviewed by local or state governments. Research funding obtained from the development of competitive proposals not only may bring in augmenting revenue but may further innovate collaborative projects. Discussion of measles outbreaks, fast-food poisoning, unintentional injuries, or sexually transmitted disease epidemics requires mastery of research principles and language.

Medical Care Setting - A health educator practicing in a medical care setting must be able to interpret and understand research findings for patients and their families as well as participate as a member of a research team that investigates behavioral components of adherence to clinical regimens. As medical care advances its technologies and treatments through the conduct of clinical trials, behavioral research becomes increasingly important in addressing chronic disease conditions and the reduction of health risk behaviors. Health educators are frequently involved in clinical research projects that further the health of the community's citizens.

School Setting - Health educators practicing in the school setting may be called upon to assist in the documentation of student health behaviors, knowledge, and attitudes. Data gained from a review of the literature and from qualitative and quantitative research endeavors are provided by health educators to school board and parents to help them understand student needs and interests. Careful use of research approaches also helps dispel intolerance relating to minority community attitudes and behaviors. Evaluation of curriculum goals, objectives, and learning activities is critical to identifying, selecting, and implementing effective curricula. Qualitative as well as quantitative research methods are increasingly being emphasized in school settings.

Workplace Setting - Adults spend the majority of their time in the work place. Health educators need both qualitative and quantitative research skills to demonstrate the efficacy of worksite health promotion programs. These research skills should address health education and promotion contributions to productivity and organizational goals. Health educators also may be asked to assist in monitoring the work environment for safety compliance and injury reduction. Additionally, by negotiating cost-effective medical care contracts, health educators may be able to help determine both quality and cost effectiveness of competing managed care plans to benefit employee medical care access.

College/University Setting - Health educators are expected to engage in scholarly endeavors that include relevant research, grant writing, and publication/dissemination of research findings. In addition to instructional and administrative responsibilities, university health educators frequently collaborate with others within and outside of their respective institutions. These efforts contribute to the scientific body of knowledge on health behavior, disease prevention, and risk reduction strategies and to the discipline of health education.

The Competencies

Competency A
Conduct a thorough review of the literature.

Competency B
Use appropriate qualitative and quantitative
research methods.

Competency C
Apply research principles to
health education practice.

AREA OF RESPONSIBILITY IX
Administering Health Education Programs

The Role

Experienced health educators often become program managers or supervisors of other health educators, or teams of allied health professionals. Good management and supervisory skills, as well as social marketing skills, require training in a variety of organizational, psychological, and business environments. Good management incorporates effective people skills, knowledge of budgeting, task assignments, and performance evaluation. Supervisors answer to higher-level management as well as to staff. These individuals require effective communication skills, organizational knowledge, and objectivity. Because of their broad training and understanding of individuals and communities, health educators can be effective managers who understand the organization which places staff in the context of larger institutional or agency issues.

Community Setting - Health educators may be responsible for managing a program of several professional and paraprofessional health educators and outreach workers who provide programs in various settings and explain health agency initiatives. More experienced health educators may advance beyond specific health education/promotion programs and find themselves directing staff in other divisions of their local public health departments, such as mental health services, environmental health services, or health planning efforts.

Medical Care Setting - Skilled health educators may be the managers of staff development programs in major medical complexes, nursing homes, or transitional facilities. The ability to communicate with a variety of medical professionals, clients, aides, volunteers, and family or community members constitutes an important management challenge. Planning programs which contribute to institutional maintenance of accreditation and compliance with government regulations also may be the task of health educators. The health educator as well may supervise institutional service- learning activities which augment staff efforts and activities.

School Setting - Advanced level health educators not only are confronted with managing classrooms of students, but they now find themselves taking on greater responsibility in identifying and securing resources to support comprehensive school health programs. Serving as curriculum coordinators or project directors, health educators may manage curricular and budgetary issues for the total school health program and may work with not-for-profit health agencies in providing selected content areas for students and staff. A frequent responsibility of the practicing health educator is the supervision of pre-service interns (student teachers). As curriculum specialists or program heads, they serve as team leaders to promote comprehensive health education in their school, throughout the school district and at the state level.

Workplace Setting - Health educators at the advanced level may find themselves in team positions as coordinators for employee assistance programs, or directors of a multi-staff health promotion effort for large corporations. As an employee, a health educator may also supervise small staff teams or contracted employees in selected health promotion programs (e.g., smoking cessation, stress management, substance misuse or weight maintenance). Supervision may include both directly employed staff and contracted staff.

College/University Setting - Health educators in this setting may be involved in a variety of administrative responsibilities, including coordination of professional preparation programs or supervision of staff in college student health centers or both. Responsibilities also might include coordinating and supervising student internships and chairing or facilitating both faculty and community committees.

The Competencies

Competency A
Develop and manage fiscal resources.

Competency B
Develop and manage human resources.

Competency C
Exercise organizational leadership.

Competency D
Obtain acceptance and support for programs.

AREA OF RESPONSIBILITY X
Advancing the Profession of Health Education

The Role

Health educators at the advanced level serve as role models for younger health educators. There are ample opportunities for professional leadership through the many professional organizations which exist to enhance the profession, advocate for individual, family and community health, and provide continuing professional education. Health educators have a responsibility to monitor, to constructively critique, and market their profession. Continuing professional education, mentoring, serving as a preceptor or supervisor, and contributing to the professional literature is the responsibility of all health educators. Health educators adhere to professional ethics at all times and demonstrate both competency and current knowledge requisite to their professional practice.

Community Setting - Health educators have the responsibility to advocate for health education and health promotion throughout community health programs. Health education is an integral part of the community and public health service delivery system; and it is up to the health educator, individually and collectively, to demand that adequate and appropriate education be a part of all activities along the human health continuum.

Medical Care Setting - Health educators must continue to advocate for the unique contributions that health education can make in medical care settings, especially at the primary care level. Physician referral to patient educators can expand patient understanding of the causes, treatments, and future prevention of illness and injury.

School Setting - Schools and school districts which embrace and implement K-12 comprehensive school health education programs in their respective buildings provide students with educational opportunities to develop life-long health enhancing behaviors. Consistently, the federal government documents the need for implementation of comprehensive school health education programs. Research shows that school-based health instruction can alter knowledge, attitudes, and health behaviors in a positive way. Within the school setting, critical issues such as interpersonal relationships, disease prevention, substance abuse, sexuality education, and violence and injury prevention can be addressed effectively in health education programs. Clearly today, families and communities along with various partnerships and coalitions participate in marketing and supporting comprehensive school health education programs. These programs are best served when advanced level health educators function in leadership roles as health advocates.

Workplace Setting - The role of health education often is overlooked in work settings. Time away from work or off the production line is seen as money lost to a company's profitability. Yet it is essential for workers to be educated about federal regulations, "workers right to know" laws, injury prevention, conflict reduction, and ways to protect their health and fitness on the job. Advocating for the profession means promoting the value of health education for adults at the worksite as well as at other settings.

College/University Setting - Health educators have the responsibility to inculcate in their students the ethical and professional underpinnings of the discipline. This may be accomplished through thesis advisement, as well as having students participate in research projects. The professionalism by which projects are completed or how students learn the process of conducting research implies that ethical principles and standards are adhered to at all times.

The Competencies

Competency A
Provide a critical analysis of current and future needs in health education.

Competency B
Assume responsibility for advancing the profession.

Competency C
Apply ethical principles as they relate to the practice of health education.

RESPONSIBILITIES AND COMPETENCIES FOR
GRADUATE LEVEL HEALTH EDUCATORS

On the following pages, the responsibilities, competencies, and sub-competencies for entry-level health educators are presented along with the additional areas of responsibility, competencies, expanded content descriptions, sub-competencies, and objectives for the graduate level health educator. Please refer to <u>A Competency-Based Framework for Professional Development of Certified Health Education Specialists</u> (NCHEC, 1996) for a complete presentation of the seven areas of responsibility of the entry-level health educator. It should be noted that a graduate level health educator is expected to be competent in all seven areas of responsibility delineated for the entry-level, in addition to the newly defined graduate level responsibilities and competencies.

Responsibilities and Competencies

RESPONSIBILITIES AND COMPETENCIES FOR ENTRY-LEVEL HEALTH EDUCATORS	ADDITIONAL RESPONSIBILITIES AND COMPETENCIES FOR GRADUATE LEVEL HEALTH EDUCATORS
I. ASSESSING INDIVIDUAL AND COMMUNITY NEEDS FOR HEALTH EDUCATION	
*Competency A: **Obtain health related data about social and cultural environments, growth and development factors, needs, and interests.***	
Sub-Competency: 1. Select valid sources of information about health needs and interests. 2. Utilize computerized sources of health-related information. 3. Employ or develop appropriate data-gathering instruments. 4. Apply survey techniques to acquire health data.	**5.** Conduct health-related needs assessment in communities. Objectives: • discuss implications of theories and models (e.g. health education, community organization, health planning) for assessment approaches • define the "community" to be assessed • compare and contrast health status indices for different population groups • using information from multiple sources, develop graphic displays of community problems

RESPONSIBILITIES AND COMPETENCIES FOR ENTRY-LEVEL HEALTH EDUCATORS	ADDITIONAL RESPONSIBILITIES AND COMPETENCIES FOR GRADUATE LEVEL HEALTH EDUCATORS
Competency B: **Distinguish between behaviors that foster and those that hinder well-being.**	
Sub-Competency: 1. Investigate physical, social, emotional, and intellectual factors influencing health behaviors. 2. Identify behaviors that tend to promote or compromise health. 3. Recognize the role of learning and affective experiences in shaping patterns of health behavior.	4. Analyze social, cultural, economic, and political factors that influence health. Objectives: • explain how social, cultural, political and economic factors influence perceptions of health • identify factors that are amenable to change • analyze factors which have a potential to impact social and individual behaviors • analyze the community's capacity to advocate, assess, plan, and achieve change
Competency C: **Infer needs for health education on the basis of obtained data.**	
Sub-Competencies: 1. Analyze needs assessment data. 2. Determine priority areas of need for health education.	

RESPONSIBILITIES AND COMPETENCIES FOR ENTRY-LEVEL HEALTH EDUCATORS	ADDITIONAL RESPONSIBILITIES AND COMPETENCIES FOR GRADUATE LEVEL HEALTH EDUCATORS
	Competency D: ***Determine factors that influence learning and development.***
	Expanded Content Description — Health educators, in the development of programs, must be able to identify, tailor and/or create materials and approaches that take into account individual learning styles, literacy capabilities, and the learning environment. Inherent in these assessments and considerations are such factors as the physical setting in which health education occurs, as well as what the learner brings to the encounter. In addition to culture, literacy and learning style, other factors are important to consider in determining readiness to learn. These would include an individual's physical and social stressors associated with health status and quality of life. These latter considerations may be particularly relevant for school-aged students. Assessing the wide variety of conditions and circumstances which can affect learning is a necessary skill for health educators.
	Sub-Competency 1: Assess individual learning styles. Objectives: • discuss theoretical concepts of learning styles • analyze different approaches to learning style assessment • select appropriate media for different learning styles • distinguish differences in approaches to pedagogy and andragogy • examine the interrelationship between health status and learning
	Sub-Competency 2: Assess individual learning literacy. Objectives: • discuss the implications of literacy for learning

RESPONSIBILITIES AND COMPETENCIES FOR ENTRY-LEVEL HEALTH EDUCATORS	ADDITIONAL RESPONSIBILITIES AND COMPETENCIES FOR GRADUATE LEVEL HEALTH EDUCATORS
	• utilize different sources for assessing literacy
	Sub-Competency 3: Assess the learning environment. Objectives: • identify physical factors that influence learning • describe social and cultural factors that influence learning • analyze the interrelationship between environmental and biological determinants of readiness to learn

II. PLANNING EFFECTIVE HEALTH EDUCATION PROGRAMS

*Competency A: **Recruit community organizations, resource people, and potential participants for support and assistance in program planning.***	
Sub-Competencies: 1. Communicate need for the program to those who will be involved. 2. Obtain commitments from personnel and decision-makers who will be involved in the program. 3. Seek ideas and options of those who will affect or be affected by the program. 4. Incorporate feasible ideas and recommendations into the planning process.	
	5. Apply principles of community organization in planning programs. Objectives: • discuss a variety of models for community organization, development and

RESPONSIBILITIES AND COMPETENCIES FOR ENTRY-LEVEL HEALTH EDUCATORS	ADDITIONAL RESPONSIBILITIES AND COMPETENCIES FOR GRADUATE LEVEL HEALTH EDUCATORS
	empowerment • explain approaches to involve local opinion leaders • describe how to recruit, train and evaluate indigenous leaders and community workers.
*Competency B: **Develop a logical scope and sequence plan for a health education program.***	
Sub-Competencies: 1. Determine the range of health information requisite to a given program of instruction. 2. Organize the subject areas comprising the scope of a program in logical sequence.	3. Review philosophical and theory-based foundations in planning health education programs. Objectives: • identify and discuss philosophical and theory-based foundations in planning health education programs • differentiate between systems and problem-solving planning approaches 4. Analyze the process for integrating health education as part of a broader health care or education program. Objectives: • describe unique characteristics of health care and education • identify ways in which programs may need to be adapted to different settings (e.g. schools, worksites, hospitals) 5. Develop a theory-based framework for health

RESPONSIBILITIES AND COMPETENCIES FOR ENTRY-LEVEL HEALTH EDUCATORS	ADDITIONAL RESPONSIBILITIES AND COMPETENCIES FOR GRADUATE LEVEL HEALTH EDUCATORS
	education programs. Objectives: • assess appropriateness of theory/models as applied to planning • select appropriate theories for program planning • modify/adapt theoretical framework/models for program planning • explain how scope and sequence of the plan is consistent with theoretical framework
Competency C: **Formulate appropriate and measurable program objectives.**	
Sub-Competencies: 1. Infer educational objectives facilitative of achievement of specified competencies. 2. Develop a framework of broadly stated, operational objectives relevant to a proposed health education program.	
Competency D: **Design education programs consistent with specified program objectives.**	
Sub-Competencies: 1. Match proposed learning activities with those implicit in the stated objectives. 2. Formulate a wide variety of alternative educational methods. 3. Select strategies best suited to implementation of educational objectives in a given setting. 4. Plan a sequence of learning	

RESPONSIBILITIES AND COMPETENCIES FOR ENTRY-LEVEL HEALTH EDUCATORS	ADDITIONAL RESPONSIBILITIES AND COMPETENCIES FOR GRADUATE LEVEL HEALTH EDUCATORS
opportunities building upon and reinforcing mastery of preceding objectives.	**5.** Select appropriate theory-based strategies in health program planning. Objectives: • describe advantages and disadvantages of various theory-based strategies • incorporate theoretical components in planning process • develop a written plan using selected models **6.** Plan training and instructional programs for health professionals. Objectives: • use adult education principles in program planning • reflect continuing professional education credentialing requirements in program design • identify current resources for continuing professional education • incorporate regulations and policy in program development, when appropriate

RESPONSIBILITIES AND COMPETENCIES FOR ENTRY-LEVEL HEALTH EDUCATORS	ADDITIONAL RESPONSIBILITIES AND COMPETENCIES FOR GRADUATE LEVEL HEALTH EDUCATORS
	Competency E: ***Develop health education programs using social marketing principles.***
	Expanded Content Description — To increase effectiveness of health education programs, reaching the intended audience is critical. Health educators continue to adapt strategies from other disciplines to improve and focus programs. Usc of strategies and techniques such as social marketing approaches assist the health educator in making certain that the characteristics of intended audiences are considered in program development and dissemination. Social marketing techniques can be very useful in more clearly delineating audience values, perceptions and beliefs, which help to improve both content and the manner of delivery.
	Sub-Competency 1: Identify populations for health education programs. Objective: • use market segmentation approaches for planning programs
	Sub-Competency 2: Involve participants in planning health education programs. Objectives: • describe methods for involving participants (e.g. observation, focus groups) • demonstrate various methods for involving participants in planning process
	Sub-Competency 3: Design a marketing plan to promote health education. Objectives: • discuss advantages/disadvantages of social marketing • employ participant data in planning • construct an approach to reach specific populations

RESPONSIBILITIES AND COMPETENCIES FOR ENTRY-LEVEL HEALTH EDUCATORS	ADDITIONAL RESPONSIBILITIES AND COMPETENCIES FOR GRADUATE LEVEL HEALTH EDUCATORS
III. IMPLEMENTING HEALTH EDUCATION PROGRAMS	
*Competency A: **Exhibit competency in carrying out planned programs.***	
Sub-Competencies: 1. Employ a wide range of educational methods and techniques. 2. Apply individual or group process methods as appropriate to given learning situations. 3. Utilize instructional equipment and other instructional media effectively. 4. Select methods that best facilitate practice of program objectives.	5. Assess, select, and apply technologies that will contribute to program objectives. Objectives: • determine the utility of various electronic innovations for education • discriminate among a variety of electronic innovations for education • use most appropriate electronic innovations to achieve stated objectives 6. Develop, demonstrate, and model implementation strategies. Objectives: • design plans of action for specific educational programs • use strategies that serve as exemplary examples

RESPONSIBILITIES AND COMPETENCIES FOR ENTRY-LEVEL HEALTH EDUCATORS	ADDITIONAL RESPONSIBILITIES AND COMPETENCIES FOR GRADUATE LEVEL HEALTH EDUCATORS
	7. Deliver educational, programs for health professionals. Objectives: • conduct training activities for selected professionals in the health field • design opportunities for information acquisition and skill development that reinforces and expands upon previous learning for professionals in the health field 8. Use community organization principles to guide and facilitate community development. Objectives: • identify ways in which community development can have an impact on implementation of health education efforts • infer a relationship between community development and health education programs • apply community empowerment and other community organization strategies to achieve health education program objectives
*Competency B: **Infer enabling objectives as needed to implement instructional program in specified settings.***	
Sub-Competencies: *asking to see if they know* 1. Pretest learners to ascertain present abilities and knowledge relative to proposed program objectives. 2. Develop subordinate measurable objectives as needed for instruction.	

RESPONSIBILITIES AND COMPETENCIES FOR ENTRY-LEVEL HEALTH EDUCATORS	ADDITIONAL RESPONSIBILITIES AND COMPETENCIES FOR GRADUATE LEVEL HEALTH EDUCATORS
Competency C: **Select methods and media best suited to implement program plans for specific learners.**	

Sub-Competencies:	
1. Analyze learner characteristics, legal aspects, feasibility, and other considerations influencing choices among methods.	
2. Evaluate the efficacy of alternative methods and techniques capable of facilitating program objectives.	
3. Determine the availability of information, personnel, time, and equipment needed to implement the program for a given audience.	
	4. Critically analyze technologies, methods, and media for their acceptability to diverse groups. Objectives: • evaluate delivery modes for their effectiveness with a selected audience. • determine appropriate delivery mode for a selected audience 5. Apply theoretical and conceptual models from health education and related disciplines to improve program delivery. Objectives: • delineate major theoretical and conceptual models from disciplines that contribute to health education, including psychology, sociology, economics, education, political

RESPONSIBILITIES AND COMPETENCIES FOR ENTRY-LEVEL HEALTH EDUCATORS	ADDITIONAL RESPONSIBILITIES AND COMPETENCIES FOR GRADUATE LEVEL HEALTH EDUCATORS
	science and anthropology • explain the relationship between theory and professional practice in health education • infer effectiveness of health education programs from theoretical and conceptual models.
Competency D: **Monitor educational programs and adjust objectives and activities as necessary.**	
Sub-Competencies: 1. Compare actual program activities with the stated objectives. 2. Assess the relevance of existing program objectives to current needs. 3. Revise program activities and objectives as necessitated by changes in learner needs. 4. Appraise applicability to resources and materials relative to given educational objectives.	

IV. EVALUATING EFFECTIVENESS OF HEALTH EDUCATION PROGRAMS

Competency A: **Develop plans to assess achievement of program objectives.**	
Sub-Competencies: 1. Determine standards of performance to be applied as criteria of effectiveness. 2. Establish a realistic scope of evaluation efforts. 3. Develop an inventory of	

RESPONSIBILITIES AND COMPETENCIES FOR ENTRY-LEVEL HEALTH EDUCATORS	ADDITIONAL RESPONSIBILITIES AND COMPETENCIES FOR GRADUATE LEVEL HEALTH EDUCATORS
existing valid and reliable tests and survey instruments. 4. Select appropriate methods for evaluating program effectiveness.	**5.** Identify existing sources of health related databases. Objectives: • access appropriate data to establish performance criteria or benchmarks for health education evaluation • determine appropriate software applications to record information for health education evaluation **6.** Evaluate existing data gathering instruments and processes. Objectives: • use selected criteria to determine appropriateness of existing evaluation instruments and processes • adapt existing evaluation instruments and processes to health education evaluation needs **7.** Select appropriate qualitative and/or quantitative evaluation design. Objectives: • compare and contrast the utility of qualitative and quantitative evaluation designs • determine an appropriate design for selected health education evaluation projects **8.** Develop valid and reliable evaluation instruments. Objectives: • explain the types of validity and reliability • describe the steps in establishing the

RESPONSIBILITIES AND COMPETENCIES FOR ENTRY-LEVEL HEALTH EDUCATORS	ADDITIONAL RESPONSIBILITIES AND COMPETENCIES FOR GRADUATE LEVEL HEALTH EDUCATORS
	validity and reliability of evaluation instruments • discuss contemporary issues about assessing validity and reliability • demonstrate use of appropriate techniques for establishing the validity and reliability of an evaluation instrument
*Competency B: **Carry out evaluation plans.***	
Sub-Competencies: 1. Facilitate administration of the tests and activities specified in the plan. 2. Utilize data collecting methods appropriate to the objectives. 3. Analyze resulting evaluation data.	4. Implement appropriate qualitative and quantitative evaluation techniques. Objectives: • demonstrate quantitative data collection techniques (e.g. conducting a survey, administering a test) • demonstrate qualitative information collection techniques (e.g. conduct a focus group, engage in participant-observation) 5. Apply evaluation technology as appropriate. Objectives: • analyze appropriateness of using evaluation technologies (e.g. audio taping, videotaping, telephone surveys, data scan forms) • describe issues involved in using evaluation technologies (e.g. informed consent, participant limitations, confidentiality)

RESPONSIBILITIES AND COMPETENCIES FOR ENTRY-LEVEL HEALTH EDUCATORS	ADDITIONAL RESPONSIBILITIES AND COMPETENCIES FOR GRADUATE LEVEL HEALTH EDUCATORS
*Competency C: **Interpret results of program evaluation.***	

Sub-Competencies: 1. Apply criteria of effectiveness to obtained results of a program. 2. Translate evaluation results into terms easily understood by others. 3. Report effectiveness of educational programs in achieving proposed objectives.	4. Implement strategies to analyze data from evaluation assessments. Objectives: • describe techniques for analyzing qualitative information and quantitative data • apply an analysis technique to evaluation data and/or information 5. Compare evaluation results to other findings. Objective: • write an analysis of findings related to previous research 6. Make recommendations from evaluation results. Objectives: • synthesize evaluation results to draw conclusions • infer future directions based on evaluation results

RESPONSIBILITIES AND COMPETENCIES FOR ENTRY-LEVEL HEALTH EDUCATORS	ADDITIONAL RESPONSIBILITIES AND COMPETENCIES FOR GRADUATE LEVEL HEALTH EDUCATORS
*Competency D: **Infer implications from findings for future program planning***	
Sub-Competencies: 1. Explore possible explanations for important evaluation findings. 2. Recommend strategies for implementing results of evaluation.	3. Apply findings to refine and maintain programs. Objectives: • critique program based on evaluation results • modify or revise the program based on evaluation findings 4. Use evaluation findings in policy analysis and development. Objectives: • determine whether findings have implications for broader policy issues • design strategies incorporating findings to influence policy development

V. COORDINATING PROVISION OF HEALTH EDUCATION SERVICES

*Competency A: **Develop a plan for coordinating health education services.***	
Sub-Competencies: 1. Determine the extent of available health education services. 2. Match health education services to proposed program activities.	

RESPONSIBILITIES AND COMPETENCIES FOR ENTRY-LEVEL HEALTH EDUCATORS	ADDITIONAL RESPONSIBILITIES AND COMPETENCIES FOR GRADUATE LEVEL HEALTH EDUCATORS
3. Identify gaps and overlaps in the provision of collaborative health services.	
Competency B: **Facilitate cooperation between and among levels of program personnel.**	
Sub-Competencies: **1.** Promote cooperation and feedback among personnel related to the program. **2.** Apply various methods of conflict reduction as needed. **3.** Analyze the role of health educator as liaison between program staff and outside groups and organizations.	
Competency C: **Formulate practical modes of collaboration among health agencies and organizations.**	
Sub-Competencies: **1.** Stimulate development of cooperation among personnel responsible for community health education programs. **2.** Suggest approaches for integrating health education within existing health programs. **3.** Develop plans for promoting collaborative efforts among health agencies and organizations with mutual interests.	
	4. Organize and facilitate groups, coalitions, and partnerships.

RESPONSIBILITIES AND COMPETENCIES FOR ENTRY-LEVEL HEALTH EDUCATORS	ADDITIONAL RESPONSIBILITIES AND COMPETENCIES FOR GRADUATE LEVEL HEALTH EDUCATORS
	Objectives: • identify strategies for building coalitions within communities • analyze issues involved in building coalitions within communities (e.g. size, funding, composition, politics) • demonstrate procedures for convening and running effective meetings • design strategies using group process skills to facilitate collaboration
*Competency D: **Organize in-service training for teachers, volunteers and other interested personnel.***	
Sub-Competencies: 1. Plan an operational, competency-oriented training program. 2. Utilize instructional resources that meet a variety of in-service training needs. 3. Develop plans for promoting collaborative efforts among health agencies and organizations with mutual interests.	4. Facilitate collaborative training efforts among health agencies and organizations. Objectives: • identify potential partners for collaboration, including criteria for selection of agencies • describe processes by which multiple organizations could be involved in training • demonstrate networking and group process skills to facilitate collaborative training

RESPONSIBILITIES AND COMPETENCIES FOR ENTRY-LEVEL HEALTH EDUCATORS	ADDITIONAL RESPONSIBILITIES AND COMPETENCIES FOR GRADUATE LEVEL HEALTH EDUCATORS

VI. ACTING AS A RESOURCE PERSON IN HEALTH EDUCATION

*Competency A: **Utilize computerized health information retrieval system effectively.***	

Sub-Competencies: 1. Match an information need with the appropriate retrieval system. 2. Access principal on-line and other database health information resources.	3. Select a data system commensurate with program needs. Objectives: • conduct comparative analysis of data sources • justify selection of sources for specific program needs 4. Determine relevance of various computerized health information resources. Objectives: • assess program's capacity to access and utilize computerized data systems • develop criteria for resource selection among several options 5. Assist in establishing and monitoring policies for use of data gathering practices. Objectives: • determine criteria for using and storing data • describe steps required to formulate an organizational data collection policy and monitoring procedures

RESPONSIBILITIES AND COMPETENCIES FOR ENTRY-LEVEL HEALTH EDUCATORS	ADDITIONAL RESPONSIBILITIES AND COMPETENCIES FOR GRADUATE LEVEL HEALTH EDUCATORS
Competency B: **Establish effective consultative relationships with those requesting assistance in solving health-related problems.**	
Sub-Competencies: 1. Analyze parameters of effective consultative relationships. 2. Describe special skills and abilities needed by health educators for consultation activities. 3. Formulate a plan for providing consultation to other health professionals. 4. Explain the process of marketing health education consultative services.	5. Apply networking skills to develop and maintain consultative relationships. Objectives: • demonstrate skills necessary for successful networking • justify the value of networking in successful consultation
Competency C: **Interpret and respond to requests for health information.**	
Sub-Competencies: 1. Analyze general processes for identifying the information needed to satisfy a request. 2. Employ a wide range of approaches in referring requesters to valid sources of health information.	

RESPONSIBILITIES AND COMPETENCIES FOR ENTRY-LEVEL HEALTH EDUCATORS	ADDITIONAL RESPONSIBILITIES AND COMPETENCIES FOR GRADUATE LEVEL HEALTH EDUCATORS
Competency D: **Select effective educational resource materials for dissemination.**	
Sub-Competencies: 1. Assemble educational material of value to the health of individuals and community groups. 2. Evaluate the worth and applicability of resource materials for given audiences. 3. Apply various processes in the acquisition of resource materials. 4. Compare different methods for distributing educational materials.	5. Apply communication theory and principles in the development of health education materials. Objectives: • describe the applicability of communication theory on the selection and development of educational materials • analyze characteristics of effective and ineffective educational materials in relation to communication theory

VII. COMMUNICATING HEALTH AND HEALTH EDUCATION NEEDS, CONCERNS, AND RESOURCES

Competency A: **Interpret concepts, purposes, and theories of health education.**	
Sub-Competencies: 1. Evaluate the state of the art	

RESPONSIBILITIES AND COMPETENCIES FOR ENTRY-LEVEL HEALTH EDUCATORS	ADDITIONAL RESPONSIBILITIES AND COMPETENCIES FOR GRADUATE LEVEL HEALTH EDUCATORS
of health education.	
2. Analyze the foundations of the discipline of health education.	
3. Describe major responsibilities of the health educator in the practice of health education.	
	4. Articulate the historical and philosophical bases of health education. Objectives: • discuss the evolution of the health education profession including major events and key people • analyze the influence of major social movements in this century on the development of the health education profession • explain the major contributions of other disciplines to the foundations of the health education discipline • defend a philosophy of health education
*Competency B: **Predict the impact of societal value systems on health education programs.***	
Sub-Competencies: 1. Investigate social forces causing opposing view-points regarding health education needs and concerns. 2. Employ a wide range of strategies for dealing with controversial health issues.	3. Analyze social, cultural, demographic and political factors that influence decision-makers.

RESPONSIBILITIES AND COMPETENCIES FOR ENTRY-LEVEL HEALTH EDUCATORS	ADDITIONAL RESPONSIBILITIES AND COMPETENCIES FOR GRADUATE LEVEL HEALTH EDUCATORS

	Objectives:
	• describe the potential influence that selected societal characteristics may have on decision makers
	• infer the role that health education can play in shaping societal values
	
	    4. Predict the future health education needs based upon societal changes.
	
	Objectives:
	• discuss emerging influences on social systems
	• conceptualize a variety of roles health education can play in responding to societal changes
	• project impact or demands on health education programs in developing new responses to societal changes
	
	    5. Respond to challenges to health education programs.
	
	Objectives:
	• explain the limitations of health education in resolving societal concerns
	• justify the value and efficacy of health education programs

Competency C: ***Select a variety of communication methods and techniques in providing health information.***	

Sub-Competencies:
 	
  1. Utilize a wide range of techniques for communicating health and health education information.
 	
  2. Demonstrate proficiency in communicating health information and health education needs.	

RESPONSIBILITIES AND COMPETENCIES FOR ENTRY-LEVEL HEALTH EDUCATORS	ADDITIONAL RESPONSIBILITIES AND COMPETENCIES FOR GRADUATE LEVEL HEALTH EDUCATORS
	3. Demonstrate both proficiency and accuracy in oral and written presentations. Objectives: • prepare a written document that provides a convincing argument in support of a complex health issue • prepare and present a public address that provides a persuasive argument in support of a complex health issue **4.** Use culturally sensitive communication methods and techniques. Objectives: • determine which means of information dissemination are effective with unique groups • design and implement an information dissemination process that is appropriate for a selected audience
Competency D: **Foster communication between health care providers and consumers.**	
Sub-Competencies: 1. Interpret the significance and implications of health care providers' messages to consumers. 2. Act as liaison between consumer groups and individuals and health care provider organizations.	

VIII. APPLY APPROPRIATE RESEARCH PRINCIPLES AND METHODS IN HEALTH EDUCATION

	Competency A: **Conduct thorough reviews of literature.**

RESPONSIBILITIES AND COMPETENCIES FOR ENTRY-LEVEL HEALTH EDUCATORS	ADDITIONAL RESPONSIBILITIES AND COMPETENCIES FOR GRADUATE LEVEL HEALTH EDUCATORS
	Expanded Content Description — Improving health education practice and increasing its social relevance requires the application of appropriate research principles and methods. An essential component of quality research is the assimilation of what has already been learned or created in the conceptualization and design of future research. Health education researchers access and critique existing literature and data sources in developing research proposals. A thorough review of attempts to answer related research questions including the approaches to gaining insight and the conclusions that have been drawn from the research are essential for quality research. Building on what has already been accomplished is inherent in making significant contributions to improving health education practice and expanding the theoretical base. **Sub-Competency 1:** Employ electronic technology for retrieving references. Objectives: • describe the range of electronic technology available for accessing information • demonstrate use of technology for a variety of purposes
	Sub-Competency 2: Analyze references to identify those pertinent to selected health education issues or programs. Objectives: • discuss the characteristics of varied information sources • determine relevance of literature to problem or programs
	Sub-Competency 3: Select and critique sources of health information. Objectives: • identify limitations and strengths of various sources of information • determine appropriateness of information

RESPONSIBILITIES AND COMPETENCIES FOR ENTRY-LEVEL HEALTH EDUCATORS	ADDITIONAL RESPONSIBILITIES AND COMPETENCIES FOR GRADUATE LEVEL HEALTH EDUCATORS
	sources based on selected criteria
	Sub-Competency 4: Evaluate the research design, methodology and findings from the literature. Objectives: • describe different research designs that have been utilized to investigate various health issues • discuss previous research methods in the development of a research proposal • compare and contrast findings from various research reports
	Sub-Competency 5: Synthesize key information from the literature. Objectives: • identify critical literature related to a selected research question • summarize the literature related to a selected research question • evaluate the applicability of previous research to a research question
	Competency B: **Use appropriate qualitative and quantitative research methods.**
	Expanded Content Description — A variety of research designs and methods are being used in research relevant to health education. The health professions in general are being challenged to use an even broader array of research methods associated with a variety of other social and behavioral disciplines. Framing a research question and using a research approach that will guide the selection of appropriate designs and methods is essential for quality research. Understanding the underlying assumptions and the strengths and weaknesses of different approaches should accompany the development of skills in quantitative or qualitative methods to conduct research.

RESPONSIBILITIES AND COMPETENCIES FOR ENTRY-LEVEL HEALTH EDUCATORS	ADDITIONAL RESPONSIBILITIES AND COMPETENCIES FOR GRADUATE LEVEL HEALTH EDUCATORS
	Sub-Competency 1: Assess the merits and limitations of qualitative and quantitative research methods. Objectives: • describe the differences in the approaches between qualitative and quantitative methods • describe epistemological assumptions underlying qualitative and quantitative designs • evaluate the merits of qualitative or quantitative approaches to a specific research question
	Sub-Competency 2: Apply qualitative and/or quantitative research methods in research designs. Objectives: • describe conditions under which a specific qualitative and/or quantitative methods would be used • design research using a qualitative and/or quantitative approach
	*Competency C: **Apply research to health education practice.***
	Expanded Content Description — Drawing inferences from research is essential for health education to continue to contribute to society. Conclusions about the significance of research findings involve the ability to interpret results in light of the roles and responsibilities of health educators. It assumes an understanding of the strengths and weaknesses of research designs and methods that have been employed. Research results are most useful when they can be applied to a range of social needs including the improvement of health education practice, the expansion of the theoretical base, the development of public policy and the shaping

RESPONSIBILITIES AND COMPETENCIES FOR ENTRY-LEVEL HEALTH EDUCATORS	ADDITIONAL RESPONSIBILITIES AND COMPETENCIES FOR GRADUATE LEVEL HEALTH EDUCATORS
	of public opinion.
	Sub-Competency 1: Use appropriate research methods and designs in assessing needs.
	Objectives:
	• discuss implications of research methods and design for needs assessment
	• apply research principles and practices in needs assessment.
	Sub-Competency 2: Use information derived from research for program planning.
	Objectives:
	• discuss implication of information derived from research for program planning
	• apply information derived from research for program planning
	Sub-Competency 3: Select implementation strategies based upon research results.
	Objectives:
	• discuss implementation strategies based upon research results
	• apply implementation strategies based upon research results
	Sub-Competency 4: Employ research design, methods and analysis in program evaluation.
	Objectives:
	• discuss research design, methods and analysis in program evaluation
	• apply research design, methods and analysis in program evaluation
	Sub-Competency 5: Describe how research results inform health policy development.
	Objective:
	• discuss conditions under which health policy is linked to research

RESPONSIBILITIES AND COMPETENCIES FOR ENTRY-LEVEL HEALTH EDUCATORS	ADDITIONAL RESPONSIBILITIES AND COMPETENCIES FOR GRADUATE LEVEL HEALTH EDUCATORS
	Sub-Competency 6: Use research results to inform health policy development. Objectives: • draft research-based policy analyses intended to encourage administrative, regulatory, or legislative changes • advocate health policy development based on research findings
	Sub-Competency 7: Use protocol for dissemination of research findings. Objectives: • identify ways to disseminate research findings • identify various procedures for dissemination of research results • prepare research reports for various constituencies

IX. ADMINISTERING HEALTH EDUCATION PROGRAMS

	*Competency A: **Develop and manage fiscal resources.***
	Expanded Content Description — When health educators move into managerial or supervisory roles, as frequently occurs in the career path of a successful advanced level health education practitioner, the responsibility for acquiring, managing, allocating and controlling fiscal resources becomes important. The health educator must have a thorough understanding of the resource allocation process within the institution and must be proficient in developing budgets, budget justifications, financial reports, and in projecting long and short-term financial needs. Development of expanded fiscal resources necessary to meet health education programming needs is a critical function and often requires that the health educator develop and pursue new funding sources, such as

RESPONSIBILITIES AND COMPETENCIES FOR ENTRY-LEVEL HEALTH EDUCATORS	ADDITIONAL RESPONSIBILITIES AND COMPETENCIES FOR GRADUATE LEVEL HEALTH EDUCATORS
	grants and contracts through federal, state and local governments, foundation awards, fee-for-service contracts with various private and public organizations, and private and community philanthropy. **Sub-Competency 1:** Prepare proposals to obtain fiscal resources through grants, contract, and other internal and external sources. Objectives: • assess fiscal needs for programs and organizations • identify internal/external sources of funding for programs • describe requirements of different funding sources • develop proposals/requests for different funders
	Sub-Competency 2: Develop and manage realistic budgets to support program requirements. Objectives: • develop budgets using appropriate software applications or other accounting methods • use appropriate accountability procedures to monitor expenditures
	*Competency B: **Develop and manage human resources.***
	Expanded Content Description — An advanced-level health educator is often responsible for supervising other employees. In order to effectively mobilize human resources to meet the program's staffing needs, a variety of skills are needed. The health educator must be thoroughly familiar with personnel rules, regulations, policies and procedures used by the agency and must, in addition, understand federal and state requirements that impinge upon the employment practices of an agency. Above and beyond the legal and administrative

RESPONSIBILITIES AND COMPETENCIES FOR ENTRY-LEVEL HEALTH EDUCATORS	ADDITIONAL RESPONSIBILITIES AND COMPETENCIES FOR GRADUATE LEVEL HEALTH EDUCATORS
	requirements, however, the effective supervisor must understand components of leadership, recognize styles of management, motivate and reward employees, and support the growth and professional development of employees. **Sub-Competency 1:** Assess and communicate qualifications of personnel needed for programs. Objectives: • identify qualifications/competencies needed for a specific position or function • construct justification for individuals to satisfy specific program needs • develop a position announcement consistent with organizational requirements
	Sub-Competency 2: Recruit, employ and evaluate staff members. Objectives: • delineate processes for attracting potential personnel • develop recruitment plan for identifying new staff or program personnel • explain personnel policies, procedures, and processes for employment of personnel (e.g. affirmative action, etc.) • identify and select appropriate instruments and procedures for personnel performance assessments
	Sub-Competency 3: Provide staff development. Objectives: • assess staff development needs • design an orientation for new personnel • design and develop opportunities for employees to increase competence • identify critical elements for effective mentoring
	Sub-Competency 4: Demonstrate leadership in managing human resources.

RESPONSIBILITIES AND COMPETENCIES FOR ENTRY-LEVEL HEALTH EDUCATORS	ADDITIONAL RESPONSIBILITIES AND COMPETENCIES FOR GRADUATE LEVEL HEALTH EDUCATORS
	Objectives: • describe various theories of leadership and management • discuss ways in which leaders can influence and motivate others to achieve program goals • explain current approaches to managing human resources
	Sub-Competency 5: Apply human resource policies consistent with relevant laws and regulations. Objectives: • identify laws, regulations, and policies that impact human resource management • discuss current applications of relevant laws, policies and regulations
	*Competency C: **Exercise organizational leadership.***
	Expanded Content Description — The health educator who moves into managerial and supervisory roles must be forward-looking, be able to articulate a clear vision for the program and be able to move the agenda of the health education program forward. This requires that the health educator understand the organizational culture in which the program functions, evaluate the political and personal influences that impact on the program's success, and be able to influence the organizational climate and to affect policy development and change, both inside and outside the organization. A basic understanding of planning concepts and methods is critical to the health educator's success. **Sub-Competency 1:** Analyze the organization's culture in relationship to program goals. Objectives: • distinguish formal and informal aspects of organizational culture

RESPONSIBILITIES AND COMPETENCIES FOR ENTRY-LEVEL HEALTH EDUCATORS	ADDITIONAL RESPONSIBILITIES AND COMPETENCIES FOR GRADUATE LEVEL HEALTH EDUCATORS
	• determine how health education influences and is influenced by organizational culture
	Sub-Competency 2: Assess the political climate of the organization, community, state and nation regarding conditions that advance or inhibit the goals of the program. Objectives: • describe political factors that influence programs • analyze sources of political pressures supporting and opposing programs • create ways of adapting programs to fit political climate
	Sub-Competency 3: Conduct long-range and strategic planning. Objectives: • describe major approaches and conceptual models used in planning • describe characteristics of long-range or strategic planning • design a strategic planning process
	Sub-Competency 4: Develop strategies to reinforce or change organizational culture to achieve program goals. Objectives: • identify factors that influence organizational culture • debate actions that may be used to change organizational culture
	Sub-Competency 5: Develop strategies to influence public policy. Objectives: • identify ways that public policy is developed and changed • describe how media is used to influence policy development • discuss the role of networking and coalition building in influencing public policy • develop and evaluate policy analysis documents

RESPONSIBILITIES AND COMPETENCIES FOR ENTRY-LEVEL HEALTH EDUCATORS	ADDITIONAL RESPONSIBILITIES AND COMPETENCIES FOR GRADUATE LEVEL HEALTH EDUCATORS
	• develop formal testimony for public hearings • draft model legislation to influence public policy
	Competency D: *Obtain acceptance and support for programs.*
	Expanded Content Description — Because health education programs may address sensitive and controversial issues, or may require long term support, it is necessary to gain acceptance and support for programs. Such acceptance and support may be required from a program administrator, school board, city council or other administrative or governing body. A health educator needs to be prepared to justify and defend programs. Such justification may be based on relevant research, or may draw on needs assessment and community advocacy. Obtaining support for programs requires knowledge of policies or regulations which relate to program content, understanding of prevailing values and beliefs within institutions and/or in various cultural groups; identification of informal and formal power structures; facility in managing public relations campaigns; and social marketing and networking skills. **Sub-Competency 1:** Apply social marketing principles and techniques to achieve program goals. Objectives: • use social marketing to promote the program • infer how social marketing can influence program acceptance • identify indicators of market response
	Sub-Competency 2: Employ concepts and theories of public relations and communications to obtain program support. Objectives: • list and describe public

RESPONSIBILITIES AND COMPETENCIES FOR ENTRY-LEVEL HEALTH EDUCATORS	ADDITIONAL RESPONSIBILITIES AND COMPETENCIES FOR GRADUATE LEVEL HEALTH EDUCATORS
	relations/communication strategies pertinent to defined audiences • write press releases and articles for lay audiences • develop media events to promote programs
	Sub-Competency 3: Incorporate demographically and culturally sensitive techniques to promote programs. Objectives: • determine the aspects of culture and demographics that influence program acceptance • construct materials appropriate for defined audiences
	Sub-Competency 4: Use needs assessment information to advocate for health education programs. Objectives: • write a program justification using needs assessment data • develop advocacy strategies which reflect needs assessment information

X. ADVANCING THE PROFESSION OF HEALTH EDUCATION

	Competency A: ***Provide a critical analysis of current and future needs in health education.***
	Expanded Content Description — Health education does not occur in a vacuum. It is a function that is intrinsically part of the larger society and is influenced by the environment in which the program exists. Health education must be responsive to social and environmental factors if it is to be successful. Understanding these factors and anticipating the impact they will have on health education needs and programming is a responsibility of the advanced-level health educator. Changing values, health status issues, health care delivery modes and

RESPONSIBILITIES AND COMPETENCIES FOR ENTRY-LEVEL HEALTH EDUCATORS	ADDITIONAL RESPONSIBILITIES AND COMPETENCIES FOR GRADUATE LEVEL HEALTH EDUCATORS
	demands on the educational system will influence the practice of health education in the future. The advanced-level health educator has an obligation to monitor changes and articulate the implications for future health education practice.
	Sub-Competency 1: Relate health education issues to larger social issues. Objectives: • describe how health education programming is influenced by social issues (e.g. issues of economy, racism, spirituality, access to care, education, poverty) • identify emerging problems that health education should be addressing
	Sub-Competency 2: Articulate health education's role in policy formation at various organizational and community levels. Objectives: • identify how policy is developed at the federal, state and local levels • define how policy development occurs in non-governmental organizations • analyze how health education can shape public opinion to influence policy development
	Competency B: ***Assume responsibility for advancing the profession.***
	Expanded Content Description — Health education practice involves more than academic preparation and competent performance. The hallmark of a professional is commitment to and support of one's profession. This can be accomplished by advocating for the profession, joining one or more professional associations, and mentoring and supporting young professionals. The role of professional associations is to advocate for issues and concerns which are held in common by professionals. The professional

RESPONSIBILITIES AND COMPETENCIES FOR ENTRY-LEVEL HEALTH EDUCATORS	ADDITIONAL RESPONSIBILITIES AND COMPETENCIES FOR GRADUATE LEVEL HEALTH EDUCATORS
	association is able to represent the aggregate membership in more visible ways than is possible for any single individual or institution. Professional associations also provide important outlets for publication and dissemination of research and for continuing professional education. Professional socialization includes knowledge of the discipline's history, understanding of the various professional specializations, and support for those bodies which have been established to speak for and about the profession. **Sub-Competency 1:** Analyze the role of the health education associations in advancing the profession. Objectives: • analyze the mission and activitics of major professional health education associations. • identify specific contributions made by health education professional associations and organizations
	Sub-Competency 2: Participate in professional organizations. Objectives: • describe various opportunities for participation in professional associations • justify which professional health education association best supports the health educator's personal career goals
	Sub-Competency 3: Develop a personal plan for professional growth. Objectives: • conduct a self-assessment of health education competencies • describe approaches for enhancing professional competencies
	*Competency C: **Apply ethical principles as they relate to the practice of health education.***

RESPONSIBILITIES AND COMPETENCIES FOR ENTRY-LEVEL HEALTH EDUCATORS	ADDITIONAL RESPONSIBILITIES AND COMPETENCIES FOR GRADUATE LEVEL HEALTH EDUCATORS
	Expanded Content Description — Ethical conduct has become a growing concern for all health professions and the behavior and conduct of health practitioners is being subjected to increasing scrutiny. Ethical dilemmas are becoming more prevalent as health education addresses a wider range of social issues. The value and utility of a health education code of ethics to individual practice and the evolution of the profession should be appreciated by practitioners. **Sub-Competency 1:** Analyze the interrelationships among ethics, values and behavior. Objectives: • differentiate among ethics, values, and behavior • hypothesize how ethics, values, and behavior affect one another
	Sub-Competency 2: Relate the importance of a code of ethics to professional practice. Objectives: • explain the major components of health education ethics • justify how a code of ethics helps shape health education as a profession
	Sub-Competency 3: Subscribe to a professionally recognized health education code of ethics. Objectives: • identify an appropriate health education code of ethics • apply a health education code to professional practice • assess options for dealing with ethical dilemmas in health education practice

APPENDIX A
Glossary*

The glossary explains terms used throughout this document. These definitions are not all-inclusive but instead are intended to convey the meaning of terms within the context of this document.

Advanced level – a point at which an individual, through experience and preparation, has mastered knowledge and skills beyond the entry-level. The advanced level professional can practice independently.

Andragogy – the methods or techniques used to teach adults.

Appropriate – suitable or compatible, fitting.

Area of responsibility – one of the major categories of performance expectations of a proficient health education practitioner. The areas of responsibility define the scope of practice.

Coalition – an alliance, often temporary, that allows two or more groups or organizations to promote a common cause.

Communication – passing on information. It involves a sender, a receiver, and a message. It can be verbal or nonverbal and is influenced by judgments, feelings, and world views (Chavez).

Communications theory – a set of constructs which attempts to explain how information is transmitted and received in a way that conveys meaning.

Community development – a broad-based effort to improve the quality of life in a geographic or social group. These efforts integrate contributions of sectors of the economy such as transportation, environment, education, and health.

Community organization – the process by which community groups are helped to identify common problems or goals, mobilize resources, and in other ways develop and implement strategies for reaching the goals they have set. Implicit in this definition is the concept of empowerment, which is viewed as an enabling process through which individuals or communities take control of their lives and their environments (Minkler).

Competency – proficiency in apply skills or in carrying out a specified task.

Conceptual model – structural designs or plans for an activity such as a health education program, which derives its justification from theoretical constructs that may be applied to a given situation.

Conflict reduction – lessening or controlling the dissonance that serves as a barrier to achieving goals.

Cultural factors – integrated pattern of human behavior that includes thought, communication, action, customs, beliefs, values and institutions of a racial, ethnic, religious, or social group (Buckner).

Culturally sensitive – implies knowledge that differences as well as similarities between and among groups exist but without making value judgments about those differences and similarities.

Demographically sensitive – acknowledging that differences in population characteristics, such as age and gender, influence program outcomes.

Effectiveness – producing an expected or desired outcome.

Entry-level – a point at which an individual has mastered the knowledge and the skills necessary to perform the minimum in core areas of responsibility and competency.

Epistemology – a branch of philosophy that investigates the origin, nature, methods and limits of human knowledge.

Ethical principles – the basic doctrine or beliefs that guide health educators in resolving dilemmas or right or wrong, good or bad, in professional decision making.

Health information – the content of communications based on data derived from systematic and scientific methods a they relate to health issues, policies, programs, services, and other aspects of individual and public health, which can be used for informing various populations and in planning health education activities (Jt. Committee on Terminology).

Health literacy – the capacity of an individual to obtain, interpret, and understand basic health information and services and the competence to use such information and services in ways that are health-enhancing (Jt. Committee on Terminology).

Learning styles – the way individuals concentrate on, absorb, and retain new and difficult information and skills (Dunn).

Needs assessment – a process by which population-based data are gathered, analyzed, and used to compare current status with that of other populations, for the purpose of improving health status within the population of focus. Effective assessment includes determination of assets available for achieving change as well as identifying gaps and deficits.

Networking – an informal process of using interconnected personal contracts to facilitate support for achievement of specific objectives.

Organizational culture – an integrated pattern of human behavior within an organization that includes thought, communication, actions, customs, beliefs, and values.

Organizational leadership – the ability to visualize the mission, to articulate a vision and to inspire actions to achieve it.

Partnership – a formal agreement of two or more individuals or organizations to engage in a shared activity.

Pedagogy – the methods or techniques used to teach children.

Profession – a group of individuals with similar educational preparation who come together for a common occupational goal and that usually exhibit the following characteristics 1) provides a unique and essential service, 2) requires of its members an extensive period of preparation, 3) has underlying its practice a theoretical base, 4) has a system of internal controls including a code of ethics that tend to regulate the behavior of its members, 5) has a culture peculiar to the profession, 6) is sanctioned by the community, and 7) has an occupational association representative of and can speak on behalf of all members of the profession (Neutens).

Professional development – the process by which an individual engages in planned activities which enhance knowledge or reinforce skills. Professional development focuses on keeping skills current and on professional growth and advancement. Terms used to describe this activity, for example, include in-service training and continuing education.

Protocol – the specification of the series of actions and sequence to be followed in executing a plan, such as a scientific study or a treatment regimen.

Public relations – the use of various communications strategies, particular over a prolonged period of time, to build good will and confidence in an organization, thereby establishing its credibility and enhancing its reputation.

Qualitative research – a type of research that applies anthropological research methods to study relevant social phenomena. Qualitative research relies on an inductive approach to understanding and is oriented toward process and discovery (Steckler).

Quantitative research – a type of research that uses methods adopted from the physical sciences, including appropriate statistical techniques, to study health behavior and other related social phenomena to determine if and to what extend predetermined study "variables" are causally related. Quantitative research is deductive in orientation and seeks verification of outcomes (Steckler).

Social marketing – a disciplined methodology for defining and promoting acceptance of socially beneficial products, behaviors, or concepts. Social marketing emphasizes demand creation for beneficial services, products, information, or practices (Favin).

Standard – the predetermined level of performance at which a criterion will be considered met. If a desired condition or characteristic (e.g. curricular content that assures development of specific health education competencies) is the criterion, the standard then expresses the minimum acceptable content that will satisfy the expectation.

Strategic planning – a disciplined effort to produce fundamental decisions and actions that shape and guide what an organization is, what it does, and why it does it. Strategic planning involves identifying organizational mandates, clarifying organizational missions and values, assessing external and internal environments, identifying strategic issues facing the organization, formulating strategies and plans to manage the issues, establishing an organizational vision, and developing an effective implementation process (Bryson).

Theory – a set of interrelated constructs (concepts), definitions, and propositions that present a systematic view of phenomena by specifying relations among variables, with the purpose of explaining and predicting the phenomena. Health education theory is derived primarily from the social and behavioral sciences, including psychology, social psychology, sociology, anthropology, economics, education and political science (Kerlinger).

Value – any belief or quality that is important, desirable, or prized (Matiella).

As developed by the Joint Committee on Graduate Standards and appended by the Graduate Competencies Writing Ad-Hoc Committee. Standards for the Preparation of Graduate-Level Health Educators (1997), published by AAHE/SOPHE.

APPENDIX B
Joint Committee for the Development of Graduate Level Preparation Standards

Committee Co-Chairpersons

Margaret M. Smith, Ed.D., CHES
Oregon State University

Stephen H. Stewart, DrPH, CHES
James Madison University

Committee Members
Evelyn E. Ames, Ph.D., CHES
Western Washington University

Donald L. Dalitri, Ed.D., CHES
Eastern Kentucky University

William Cissell, Ph.D., CHES
Texas Woman's University

Patricia P. Evans, MPH
Council on Education for Public Health

Mary E. Hawkins, MSPH, M.Ed., CHES
North Carolina Central University

Douglas Hippler
Parkway Center Senior High School

Mark J. Kittleson, Ph.D.
Southern Illinois University at Carbondale

William C. Livingood, Jr., Ph.D., CHES
East Stroudsburg University

Captain Patricia D. Mail, MPH, CHES
National Commission for Health Education Credentialing, Inc.

Carl J. Peter, Ph.D., CHES
Western Illinois University

Donald A. Read, Ed.,D.
Worcester State College

Ruth Richards, M.A., MPH
University of California at Los Angeles

James Robinson, III, Ph.D., CHES
Texas A&M University

Elaine M. Vitello, Ph.D., CHES
Southern Illinois University at Carbondale

Support Staff

Aileen M. Frazee, M.Ed.
Association for the Advancement
of Health Education

APPENDIX C
Members of the
Graduate Competencies Implementation Committee

Elaine Auld
Society for Public Health Education

Ellen M. Capwell
Ohio Department of Health

William B. Cissell
Texas Women's University

William B. Cosgrove
National Commission for Health Education
Credentialing

Pat Evans
Council on Education for Public Health

Aileen Frazee
American Association for Health Education

Gary D. Gilmore
University of Wisconsin

Audrey Gotsch
UMDNJ-RW Johnson Medical School

William C. Livingood
University of North Florida

Sheila M. Patterson
West Chester University

James Robinson
Texas A & M University

Louis Rowitz
University of Illinois at Chicago

Becky J. Smith
American Association for Health Education

Margaret Smith
Salem, OR

Stephen II. Stewart
James Madison University

Alyson Taub
New York University

Elaine M. Vitello
Southern Illinois University

APPENDIX D
Members of the
Graduate Competencies Writing Ad-Hoc Committee

Pat Evans
Council on Education for Public Health

William C. Livingood
East Stroudsburg University

Patricia Mail
National Commission for Health Education Credentialing, Inc.

James Robinson
Texas A & M University

Margaret Smith
Oregon State University

Alyson Taub
New York University

APPENDIX E
Information About The Organizations

AMERICAN ASSOCIATION FOR HEALTH EDUCATION
1900 Reston Drive
Reston, VA 20191
Phone: 800/213-7193
Web Site: www.aahperd.org/aahe/aahe.html

The mission of the American Association for Health Education (AAHE) is to advance the profession while serving health educators and other professionals who strive to promote the health of all people. AAHE is a membership organization representing 7,500 health educators and health promotion specialists and is the oldest and largest health education association. AAHE is one of six national associations in the American Alliance for Health, Physical Education, Recreation, and Dance, which is divided into six multiple state geographical sub-organizations called districts.

NATIONAL COMMISSION FOR HEALTH EDUCATION CREDENTIALING
944 Marcon Blvd, #310
Allentown, PA 18103
Phone: 888/624-3248
Web site: www.nchec.org

The mission of the National Commission for Health Education Credentialing, Inc., is to improve the quality of health education practice through the establishment, implementation and maintenance of a certification process for health education specialists and through the promotion of scientific, ethical and state-of-the-art programs of professional preparation and continuing education. NCHEC has certified over 6200 individuals since 1989.

SOCIETY FOR PUBLIC HEALTH EDUCATION
1015 Fifteenth St, NW, #410
Washington, DC 20005
Phone: 202/408-9804
Web site: www.sophe.org

The Society for Public Health Education (SOPHE) is an independent international professional organization founded in 1950 to provide leadership to the profession of health education and to contribute to the health of all people through: 1) advances in health education theory and research; 2) excellence in health education practice; and 3) promotion of public policies conducive to health. SOPHE has some 4,000 national and local members in 18 chapters and 20 foreign countries.

REFERENCES

American Association for Health Education. (May/June,1991). Report of the 1990 Joint Committee on Health Education Terminology, *Journal of Health Education*, 28(5), 173-183.

American Association for Health Education/Society for Public Health Education. (1997). Standards for the preparation of graduate-level health educators. Washington, DC.

American Association for Health, Physical Education and Recreation. (1969). Recommended standards and guidelines for teacher preparation in health education. *Health Education* 40(2), 31-38.

American Association for Health, Physical Education and Recreation. (1974). Professional preparation in safety education and school health education. Report of a National Conference on Undergraduate Professional Preparation. Washington, DC.

American Public Health Association. Committee on Professional Education. (March, 1969). Criteria and guidelines for accrediting graduate programs in community health education. *American Journal of Public Health* 59(3), 534-542.

American School Health Association. (1976). Professional preparation of the health educator. Kent, OH.

Athletic Institute. (1950). Report on the national conference on graduate study in health education, physical education, and recreation. Chicago, IL.

Association for the Advancement of Health Education. (1994). Code of ethics for health educators. *Journal of Health Education*. 25(4), 197-200.

Association for the Advancement of Health Education. (May/June 1996). AAHE name change. *HE-Xtra* 21(3):1.

Bensley, L.B. and Pope, A.J. (1992). A self-study instrument for program review of graduate programs in health education. *Journal of Health Education* 23(6), 344-346.

Bryson, John M. (1995). Strategic Planning for Public and Nonprofit Organizations. San Francisco, CA: Jossey Bass Publishers.

Buckner, W.P. Jr. (1994). "Promoting Multicultural Sensitivity Among Educators." In Cortese, P., & Middleton, K. (Eds.), Comprehensive School Health Challenge: Promoting Health Through Education Vol II. Santa Cruz, CA: ETR Associates.

Chavez, G. (1989). La Communicacion. Santa Cruz, CA: Network Publications.

Dunn, R. (1983). Learning style and its relation to exceptionality at both ends of the spectrum. *Exceptional Children 49*, (6), pp 496-506.

Cleary, H.P. (1995). The credentialing of health educators: An historical account 1970-1990. National Commission for Health Education Credentialing, Inc., New York.

Creswell, W.H. (1981). Professional preparation: An historical perspective. Pages 43-60 in U.S. Department of Health and Human Services (Ed.), National Conference for Institutions Preparing Health Educators. Department of Health and Human Services, Washington, DC.

Favin, M. and Griffiths, M. Social Marketing of Micronutrients in Developing Countries. The OMNI Project Report. Arlington, VA: John Snow, Inc.

Henderson, A. and McIntosh, D. (1981). Role refinement and verification for entry-level health educators. (HRP 0904273) National Center for Health Education, San Francisco, CA.

Joint Committee for Graduate Standards. (1997). Proceedings of National Congress for Institutions Preparing Graduate Health Educators. AAHE and SOPHE, Reston, VA.

Kerlinger, F.N. (1986). Foundations of Behavioral Research. New York: Rinehard & Winston.

Mail, P. (1997). Standardizing professional preparation: Extending the process to graduate education, Proceedings of National Congress for Institutions Preparing Graduate Health Educators, 72-84. AAHE and SOPHE, Reston, VA.

Mathews, B. (1983). A guide for the development of competency-based curricula for entry-level health educators. National Task Force on the Preparation and Practice of Health Educators, Inc., New York.

Matiella, A., (1988). Cultural Pride. Santa Cruz, CA: ETR Associates, Network Publications.

Minkler, M. (1990). Improving Health Through Community Organization. In K. Glanz, et al. (ed), Health Behavior and Health Education: Theory, Research and Practice, 257-287. San Francisco: Jossey Bass Publishers.

National Task Force on the Preparation and Practice of Health Educators. (1985). A framework for the development of competency-based curricula for entry-level health educators. New York.

National Commission for Health Education Credentialing. (1996). A competency-based framework for professional development of certified health education specialists. New York.

Neutens, J. (1984). Professional Competencies of the Health Educator. In rubinson, L. and Alles, W. (Eds.), Health Education Foundations for the Future. Prospect Heights, IL: Waveland Press.

Society for Public Health Education/Ad Hoc Task Force on Professional Preparation and Practice of Health Education. (1977). Guidelines for the preparation and practice of professional health educators. *Health Education Monographs* 5(1), 75-89.

Society for Public Health Education. (1967). Board of Directors meeting minutes, March 14, 1967.

Society for Public Health Education. (1983). SOPHE Code of Ethics, Berkeley, CA.

U.S. Department of Health, Education and Welfare, Health Resources Administration, Bureau of Health Manpower. (1978). Preparation and practice of community, patient, and school health educators: Proceedings of the Workshop on Commonalties and Differences. Division of Allied Health Professions, Washington, DC.

U.S. Department of Health and Human Services. (1980). Initial role delineation for health education: Final report. (DHHS Publication No. HRA 80-44). U.S. Government Printing Office, Washington, DC.

U.S. Department of Health and Human Services. (1981). National Congress for Institutions Preparing Health Educators. (DHHS Publication No. 81-50171). Government Printing Office, Washington, DC.

Notes

1. SOPHE no longer requires an MPH as a requirement for membership.

2. Cleary (1995) notes that there was considerable disagreement as to whether "entry-level" should be at the baccalaureate or masters level. Since that time, the proliferation of baccalaureate programs has created the perception that "entry-level" is synonymous with a bachelor's preparation. This perception may have kept graduate programs from utilizing the Framework and encouraging their students to seek certification. In fact, "entry-level" was the term used to denote an individual who was "innocent of any preparation in health education" until he or she had completed a course of training, preferably one that adhered to a competency-based curriculum. Entry-level was meant to denote the person who was new to the profession, even though he or she might already be qualified and certified in another allied health or other profession.

3. At the annual meeting of AAHE in 1996, the Board of Directors voted to change the name of the Association for the Advancement of Health Education to the American Association for Health Education (AAHE, 1996).

4. No effort was made to change the existing framework in deference to the National Commission for Health Education Credentialing.